Discovering
EPITAPHS

Geoffrey N. Wright

Shire Publications Ltd.

CONTENTS

PHOTOGRAPHS

Photographs are acknowledged as follows: John Bland, plates 10, 14, 19; Courtney Dainton, plate 5; Cadbury Lamb, plate 17; John A. Long, plate 12; Frances Rivington, plate 11; David Uttley, plate 2; J. W. Whitelaw, plates 6, 8, 18; Geoffrey N. Wright, plates 1, 3, 4, 7, 9, 13, 15, 16; Mrs. E. Preston, plate 20.

Note. This book was first published before the reorganisation of local government in 1974 and the counties to which places are ascribed in the text and gazetteer refer to the boundaries prevailing before that date.

Printed in Great Britain by C. I. Thomas & Sons (Haverfordwest) Ltd, Press Buildings, Merlins Bridge, Haverfordwest.

INTRODUCTION

Our churchyards are one of our priceless and unique heritages. They contain a rich and relatively untapped source of vernacular art in which imaginative skill and craftsmanship in lettering, sculpture, and the use of local materials have combined to produce an almost infinite range of memorials, the like of which cannot be found in any other country. Generations of our ancestors are commemorated quietly, expansively, sadly, humorously, whimsically, eccentrically, and quite often anonymously.

Epitaphs, embellishments and inscriptions on churchyard memorials record the frailty of human life—and its continuity; they tell us how previous generations have lived, and what they believed—they are mirrors of the contemporary social scene. There is a whole social history recorded in epitaphs, for they also tell us about the trades, occupations, and professions of the people who lived in a particular district at a particular time.

The churchyard—especially the country churchyard—has become part of our life and our landscape. Each example of it has been individually created by men and by time. In Saxon times it was defined as 'God's acre', but in the Middle Ages it served as the village meeting-place, for fairs and other communal activities, so perhaps after all it is quite appropriate that the churchyard should be the place where local talents and skills found their natural outlet in sculpture, epitaph, and verse.

There are thousands of churchyards in this country, most of them with dozens—sometimes hundreds—of gravestones. This book does not set out to be a comprehensive summary, but merely seeks to arouse the interest and whet the appetite of the reader, to encourage him or her to explore these storehouses of history and human frailty for himself.

1. HISTORICAL BACKGROUND

The earliest Christian monuments in this country took one of two forms: either a horizontal slab placed across two uprights, as in pagan burial-places, or a simple, upright stone by itself. The first memorials with dedicatory inscriptions were introduced to this country during the Roman occupation and many of these can be seen in museums at important Romano-British sites such as York, Colchester and Cirencester, and at the British Museum in London.

During the Dark Ages which followed the Roman occupation Christian grave memorials reached a very high standard of decoration. Celtic and Saxon carved crosses and decorated grave-slabs are evidence of great skills in sculpture and design, as traditional in their day as are those of succeeding craftsmen several centuries later.

In parish churches the earliest tombs are those from the twelfth century, which take the form of simple stone slabs commemorating church dignitaries, who were the only people allowed to be buried in the church. The following century saw the appearance of the recumbent effigy of the lord of the manor. Inscriptions on these tombs were in Latin, which together with the dress, armour and heraldry of the effigy add to our knowledge of that century. In the fourteenth century came finely carved stone canopies over the recumbent effigies; the making of these was an important source of employment.

Throughout the Middle Ages it was only the wealthy who had memorials. The poor did without; they were simply buried in the churchyard, one on top of another, over the centuries. This custom has raised the level of old churchyards several feet above the ground outside as well as covering the lower courses of the walls of the church itself. The 'moat' which sometimes surrounds a church, separating it from the adjoining churchyard, has been dug to reduce the drainage problem thereby produced. Kenneth Lindley has pointed out that with an average of only six burials a year a churchyard which has been in use for 800 years has 4,800 bodies stacked around it! The oldest graves in a churchyard are to the south of the church, as it was desirable to avoid the church's shadow falling across them. The Devil lurked among shadows and was always supposed to enter a churchyard from the north; hence for many years the north side was not used for burials—at least not until the south side could take no more.

Churchyard tombstones came into common use from the earliest years of the seventeenth century onwards. The reason is a social and economic one. The Elizabethan age had seen England develop into a prosperous nation. This prosperity moved down the social scale and created a middle class between the very wealthy, who became even richer, and the very poor, who became slightly less poor. The middle classes could afford the luxury of commemorative monuments, and as they grew more wealthy their monuments became more splendid; as they became more numerous, so did their memorials.

The earliest memorials in churchyards, some of which still bear decipherable inscriptions, were probably made by general masons—men whose skill with stone was more commonly used in building houses, barns, and walls. The rich variety of inventive design in these memorials reflects the instinctive and inherited approach to design, as well as a familiarity with the working materials, possessed by these skilled craftsmen.

Monumental masonry as a trade probably originated in late seventeenth or early eighteenth centuries and was basically a rural business primarily concerned with the use of local materials. It developed during the eighteenth century, and was influenced by new styles of design, and particularly Classical architecture. Books on design and decoration had been published, including Thomas Chippendale's *The Gentleman and Cabinet-Maker's Director* in 1754, which contained engravings of various motifs suitable for use on furniture, but which could without much difficulty have provided masons with ideas translatable to stone.

The Adam brothers, Robert and James, produced their famous book on architecture in 1773. Its influence and the subsequent dominance of what was called the 'Adam style' was also reflected in monumental sculpture, in urns, sprays, draperies and simple decorations, which lasted until the mid nineteenth century. By then the mass-produced article had appeared and catalogues of designs were available to monumental masons, who merely added inscriptions to prefabricated monuments.

2. SHAPES AND SYMBOLS

Memorial stones of the late sixteenth and early seventeenth centuries are usually short, dumpy, thick upright slabs, carved on one side only. Burials were orientated east-west, with the head at the west so that the eyes could face the rising sun. Headstones were usually at the head or western end of the tomb, with the carved side to the east. This is not always the case, although in each individual churchyard there tends to be uniformity—all the carved faces are to the east, or all are to the west (as I have sometimes discovered in parts of Scotland). The worked face to the east does give extra protection to the carving by keeping it away from the prevailing wind—an important factor where memorials were of a soft stone, as in the Cotswolds.

Headstones were originally intended to carry only one inscription, but were soon expected to include the names of other members of the family buried subsequently, so that one headstone might finish up bearing ten or more names, occasionally with an overflow to the reverse side.

Headstones developed in outline through the seventeenth century, becoming larger in area and thinner in section. By the next century refinements in design, brought about by specialism in monumental masonry, were reflected in improved lettering and decoration, at first on the simple rectangular shape and later on upright slabs with curved, scrolled, and indented tops, adding their variety of silhouette to the churchyard scene.

The oldest and commonest form of memorial after headstones is the simple horizontal slab, called a ledger. At first this was a flat stone several inches thick laid lengthwise above the body so that its surface coincided with ground level. Their heavy weight has made many of these gradually sink, so that they are now themselves buried beneath the surface. Ledger stones, by their size and weight, discouraged potential grave-robbers or body-snatchers but they suffered from the encroachment of surrounding vegetation, so modifications became necessary. Ledger stones were raised on four legs to create table tombs with infilled sides, similar to those that had long been used inside churches, particularly as a base on which to support effigies. Such tombs are hollow and, where the sides are filled in, extra surfaces become available for inscriptions and decoration, an aspect taken great advantage of by monumental masons in a variety of ways.

The proportions of most table or altar tombs are those of

the double cube—that is, two cubes adjacent to each other—but in the Cotswolds around **Burford** a rather more narrow version become popular, surmounted by a 'Swiss-roll' top, scalloped at each end, and usually with a skull placed at the centre of the scallop. These are known as bale tombs—possibly by association of ideas, for the shape of the top is supposed to represent a bale of wool and many of these tombs commemorate Cotswold wool merchants (plate 1).

Whereas table tombs emphasize length, pedestal tombs accentuate height, being based on a square podium and capped appropriately by a pediment of some Greek or Roman 'order'. The most frequent form of podium has an urn on top, which, draped or not, is the commonest churchyard feature of the eighteenth century onwards. A more grandiose decoration on a podium is the obelisk.

Painswick churchyard (plate 2) has a splendid collection of pedestal-type monuments—square, circular, octagonal, with straight or sometimes concave faces and corners ornamentally buttressed. Most of them are tombs of local merchant families and date from the late eighteenth century. Other villages along the lower Severn valley also have this tradition of pedestal tombs with splendidly varied imagery, many of them the work of local monumental masons in the early nineteenth century. One such mason was John Pearce, of **Frampton-on-Severn,** whose characteristic trade-mark on a tomb was a drooping sheaf of foliage above the inscription contained within an oval inset. Pyramid tombs represent the ultimate in pedestal type, but are far less common, perhaps because of their pagan associations. Oddly enough, the mason who produced much of the fine work at Painswick has a plain pyramid above his own grave.

As a grave memorial the now familiar cross did not appear in any quantity until the second half of the nineteenth century. Its popularity has steadily increased mainly because it is the cheapest memorial to make. Variations on it include the imitation Celtic cross (with a circle around the cross itself), the cross-with-anchor, very common in seaside graveyards, and the cross-with-angel.

Wooden memorials were common during the seventeenth century in Surrey and the Weald, and in other parts of the Home Counties where there is little local stone. These graveboards consist of a wooden rail fixed between two uprights or supported on two crucks. **High Easter** churchyard, Essex, has a grave with two oak headposts showing the remains of carving, while a more weathered example is at **Little Easton** nearby. **Rendlesham,** Suffolk, also has an eighteenth century wooden graveboard, and the oldest one yet discovered and deciphered is at **Sidlesham,** Sussex, where a square wooden beam shows lettering on two faces to Thomas Greenwood (1658).

3. MATERIALS

Slate is in many ways the ideal material for headstones. It is very durable, it weathers well, and it is easy to work. Those parts of the country which have slate quarries—Cornwall, North Wales, the Lake District, and Leicestershire with adjoining parts of Staffordshire and Nottinghamshire—are regions where the churchyards are rich in splendid headstones, superbly embellished and beautifully lettered.

Although the earliest slates appeared as headstones in the seventeenth century their great period of use was from the early eighteenth century right through to the mid nineteenth, when they ceased to be used, mainly because the quarries, especially those of the Midlands, were worked out. Other slate quarries were still in production however, and improved transport has resulted in slate headstones appearing in places far removed from their source of origin.

Stone of some sort is available in almost every part of the country, and until the development of canals and railways from 1780 onwards headstones were made from stone quarried locally, though some Dorset and Yorkshire stone, quarried near the coast, was transported to other areas by sea. Some local stones, like those of the Cotswolds, carve well but weather very badly. Cotswold masons realising this, set brass plaques into the stone for epitaphs and other inscriptions. Other metals were used for this purpose, and **Lavenham** and **Long Melford** in Suffolk have good eighteenth-century examples, while **Beckley,** Oxfordshire, has a stone with a cherub's head in lead.

Metal memorials have the undoubted virtue of indestructibility. Places where iron-founding was an important local trade have many cast iron memorials in their churchyards. There are some cast iron grave-slabs inside **Wadhurst** church, Sussex, which date from 1614 to 1790. Similar iron grave-slabs are at **Rotherfield** and **East Grinstead,** Sussex, and **Crowhurst,** Surrey. **Leiston** and **Long Melford,** Suffolk, have slabs made by local iron-founders, while in the same county, **Westleton** has two fine cast iron 'head and foot' pairs of memorials. But the greatest iron-founders were in Shropshire and in that county, especially around **Coalbrookdale,** the most cast iron monuments are found. **Madeley** churchyard has a splendid collection, including a number of cast iron table tombs and others of the pedestal type surmounted by a small decorative urn. In most cases lettering on these iron grave-slabs is in relief, though sometimes it is incised on a bolted-on panel. Iron foundries did exist in a number of quite small country towns last century outside the normal iron-founding areas, and it is not uncommon to find occasional iron memorials in village churchyards in the vicinity.

Until white Italian marble came into its own in this country it was common practice to paint headstones—usually the incised letters being given a colour contrasting strongly with the surrounding stone. Backgrounds and decorations were painted red, blue, yellow or green, with occasional gilt. There are some good examples inside the church at **Llanvetherine** in Monmouthshire and a restored collection at **Compton Beauchamp,** Berkshire. But the very best set of painted headstones is not in a churchyard at all, but adorns the outside wall of a monumental mason's yard at **Great Bedwyn,** a few miles from Marlborough, Wiltshire (plates 4 and 9).

---

4. INSCRIPTIONS AND EPITAPHS

Most of the identifiable and still-legible inscriptions on churchyard memorials date from the seventeenth century or later. Those of the seventeenth century are usually brief and factual, but in the eighteenth and nineteenth centuries they become more verbose, sometimes ingenious, often vainglorious, tender or brutal, sublime or ridiculous, and not infrequently remarkably witty.

The College of Arms was the body officially responsible for supervising heraldry and epitaphs, but its authority declined from the early part of the seventeenth century. Weever, writing in 1631, suggested that an epitaph should consist of 'the name, the age, the deserts, the dignities, the state, the praises both of body and mind, the good or bad fortunes in the life, and the manner and time of the death, of the person therein interred'. Camden had earlier argued that an epitaph should 'show love to the deceased, memory to posterity, and comfort to friends'. Later Fuller preferred that 'the shortest, the plainest, and truest are the best'.

Had the present standardised inscriptions on memorials

been all that was permitted in centuries past, churchyards would be far less interesting places and social historians would be much worse off for information about the lives of ordinary people. A random collection of epitaphs throws a great deal of light upon the customs and attitudes of our ancestors, revealing not only something of their personalities, but also mirroring the spirit of the times in which they lived.

Right down to the latter part of the nineteenth century much of the verse and inscriptions on churchyard memorials was concerned with the fact of mortality, its inevitability, and its levelling powers. Thus the moral expressed, in different forms, in the commonest of epitaphs:

> As you are now; so once was I;
> As I am now; so you shall be;
> Therefore prepare to follow me.

From **Bury St. Edmunds,** Suffolk, a stone now transferred to the wall of the ruined charnel-house commemorates Sarah Worton, who died in 1698:

> Good people all as you
> Pas by, looke round
> See how Corpes' do lye
> For as you are, som time Ware We
> and as we are so must you be

A slate, beautifully maintained, at **Hickling,** Nottinghamshire, and dated 1727, has this verse:

> You readers all both old and young
> Your time on earth will not be long
> For death will come and die you must
> And like to me return to dust.

Also in Nottinghamshire, at **Farndon** (1757):

> Stay mortal and depart not from my stone,
> But stand and Ponder well where I am gone
> Death quickly took me sense and strength away
> And laid me down upon this Bed of Clay.
> Consider of it and take Home this Line
> The Grave that is made next may chance be Thine.

From one end of the country to the other these grim warnings to our seventeenth and eighteenth century ancestors are repeated. **Widecombe-in-the-Moor,** Devon, has a charming version of 1776:

> The Rose is red: ye Gras is green: the Days are past which I have seen. All ye on me Cast & Eye: as you are now So once was I but as I am now so shall ye be Pre pare for Death and follow me.

In Scotland the lament is louder, the warning grimmer. A

number of very fine stones of red sandstone, beautifully lettered and embellished, can be found in churchyards in Galloway, where these, or similar lines, occur on a number of eighteenth-century memorials. The one quoted is from **Anwoth**, near Gatehouse of Fleet:

> Hark from the Tomb a doleful sound
> My Ears attend the Cry
> Ye living Men come view the Ground
> Where you must shortly ly.

It soon becomes obvious when surveying such epitaphs and inscriptions of seventeenth and eighteenth century memorials that there is an almost complete absence of any statement of Christian faith. This partly arose from an underlying fear of popery and partly from a characteristic British trait of displaying no outward show of religious fervour. By the turn of the century an increasing emphasis on salvation by means of faith becomes apparent, possibly due to Methodist influences, and possibly to the increasingly educational value of the Sunday-school movement. A 'warning' epitaph of 1874 from **Broadway**, Worcestershire, illustrates the christianising element in its last line:

> My time is come. Next may be thine
> Prepare for it whilst thou has time
> And that thou mayst prepared be
> Live unto Him who died for thee.

Masham, Yorkshire, has an example typifying this change of attitude from fatalism to salvation, dated 1809:

> My friends, read this and shed no tears
> I must lay here till Christ appears
> And at His coming hope to have
> A joyful rising from the Grave.

Death after illness

Outbreaks of plague ceased only as late as the middle of the seventeenth century, but they were followed by epidemics of cholera and smallpox, which, in the virtual absence of any preventive medicine, caused a high mortality rate. In addition very poor diet led to tuberculosis or consumption, and many epitaphs exist which are reminders of deaths following long or short illnesses. Occurring all over the country is the quatrain:

> Afflictions sore long time I bore
> Physicians were in vain
> Till God did please Death should me seize
> And ease me of my pain.

A stone at **Painswick,** Gloucestershire, of 1799, tells of a sudden death, presumably by heart attack:

> As through the fields he walk'd alone,
> By chance he met grim death;
> Who with his dart did strike his heart,
> And robb'd him of his breath.

Mentioning the disease by name is the oft-recurring epitaph:

> A pale consumption gave the final blow.
> The stroke was fatal, though th' effect came slow.

The appalling infant mortality rate of the eighteenth and nineteenth centuries needs no verses to pinpoint its grim terrors. Simple statements of hard, cold fact on stone after stone are all the evidence necessary. Many tombs merely record, with the death of one or other of the parents, the names and ages of their children also buried there. The lonely churchyard of **Cartmel Fell**, Lancashire, commemorates Isabella Taylor, who died in 1878, Ann, fourth daughter, who died in 1869 aged 16, and Jane, Isaac, Thamer, Wilson and Joseph, all of whom died in infancy. At **Easton-in-Gordano**, Somerset, is the grave of one Harriet Pains, died 1850 aged 10, together with fourteen of her brothers and sisters who died in infancy. But saddest of all must be the stone to Rebecca Town, of **Keighley,** Yorkshire, who died in 1851 aged 44, of whose thirty children only one reached the age of three years, the rest dying in infancy.

Longevity on gravestones

At the other end of the scale there are a remarkable number of examples of longevity, many recorded on gravestones. At **Bolton-on-Swale,** a few miles from Northallerton, Yorkshire, a churchyard tomb commemorates the oldest of them all, one Henry Jenkins, said to have lived to the age of 169 years. This astonishing achievement has gained for him a place in the *Dictionary of National Biography.* Born about 1501, he could remember having been sent as a boy to Northallerton with a load of arrows at the time of the battle of Flodden (1513); he visited the last abbot of Fountains Abbey; shortly before he died he appeared as a witness at York Assizes, deposing in evidence his knowledge that certain tithes of wool and lamb had been paid 120 years previously! A tablet to his memory was placed inside the church in 1743, 73 years after his death, and carries a very long epitaph. The churchyard tomb was erected by public subscription.

An unsolved mystery surrounds the grave of **Thomas Newman**, in the churchyard of St. Luke's, **Brislington**, Bristol.

This stone reads:

> 1542 THOMAS NEWMAN Aged 153. This stone was new faced in the year 1771 to Perpetuate the Great Age of the Deceased.

And in the south aisle of the Priory Church in **Bridlington,** Yorkshire, is a board with this inscription painted on it:

> 1542. Thomas Newman Aged 153 years. This stone was refaced in 1771 to preserve the recollection of this remarkable prolongation of human life.

The stone in Bridlington churchyard has disappeared. It would be stretching coincidence too far to suppose there were two Thomas Newmans who each lived to 153, and who each died in 1542. The Brislington grave is of a Bath stone used locally before the Pennant stones used elsewhere in the churchyard and is much softer than them, so it was probably necessary to reface it by 1771. It is highly unlikely that anyone would steal and transport a stone from Bridlington to Bristol, and since the Bristol stone exists and the one at Bridlington does not, perhaps its validity is less open to question!

Other records of longevity include the famous case of 'Old Parr'—Thomas Parr of Great Willaston, Cheshire, who died in Shropshire in 1635 at the age of 152, and is buried in **Westminster Abbey.** Thomas Damme, a native of Chester, died aged 154; Isaac Ingall, butler of **Battle Abbey,** Sussex, reached a mere 120 years. **Stoke-on-Trent** churchyard has the graves of Henry and Sibil Clarke, who both died in 1684 aged 112. The epitaph of Matthew Peat at **Wirksworth,** Derbyshire, who died in 1751 aged 112, poses the question: 'Few live so long: who lives well?' Sarah Jarvis of **Corsham,** Wiltshire, who died in 1753 aged 107, had, some time before her death, 'a third set of teeth'.

The social content of even brief epitaphs to people who had lived to a great age is often worth noting: William Billinge, of **Longnor,** Staffordshire, was born in a cornfield, served at Gibraltar and Ramillies and died in 1791 aged 112. Joseph Watson, keeper of a deer-park, was buried at **Disley,** Cheshire, and is recorded as being 'the first that perfected the art of driving stags'. He lived to 104, as did Annie Abraham, of **Kilmersdon,** Somerset, whose epitaph stated that until two years before her death in 1849 she walked regularly to her work, a distance of 1½ miles.

Husbands and wives

One of the most famous epitaphs to a wife can scarcely be said to praise her. The great pity is that the original stone bearing these lines in **Potterne** churchyard, near Devizes, Wiltshire, has vanished. The epitaph is quoted from the famous book of Thomas Ravenshawe's published in 1878, *Antiente Epitaphes,* in which the date of the stone is given as 1790:

> Here lies MARY the Wife of JOHN FORD,
> We hope her soul is gone to the LORD;
> But if for Hell she has chang'd this life,
> She had better be there than be John Ford's wife.

This does not say much for her husband either! Less condemning, but speaking volumes no doubt, this epitaph from **Troutbeck,** Westmorland has also achieved some fame:

> Here lies a woman,
> No man can deny it,
> She died in peace, although she lived unquiet,
> Her husband prays, if e'er this way you walk,
> You would tread softly—if she wake she'll talk.

The simple honesty of the early eighteenth century is typified in an all-embracing manner by this epitaph from **Brightlingsea,** Essex, where a ledger stone has these words:

> Under these clods lyeth the Dodds.
> Four Children here the Earth Encloseth
> Elizabeth John Sarah and Joseph
> Likewise their mother Sarah Dodd
> Whose Soul I hope doth rest with God
> My Wife the 4th Day of October (1728)
> This painful life she did give over
> And unto Death her breath did yield
> When fifty seven years were fill'd.
> Here lies enclosed Elias Dodd
> His Wife and Children Small
> I hope they rest among the Blest
> And Pray God Save us all.

From **Wistanstow,** Shropshire, comes this epitaph of a woman who died at the age of 77. Was it mathematical vanity, or merely the feminine wish to hide her age, that resulted in this.

> Twice six, twice seven,
> Twice twenty, and eleven.

Nicholas Toke, buried at **Great Chart,** Kent, has on his stone:

> He married five wives whom he survived. At the age of 93 he walked to London to seek a sixth but died before he found her.

Two adjacent tombs at **Birdbrook,** Essex, can cap this:

> Martha Blewitt ye wife of nine husbands successively, buried 8 of ym, but last of all, ye woman dyed allsoe, was buryed May 7, 1681.

and:

> Robert Hogand, the husband of seven wives, the last
> of whom he married January 1st 1739.

The talkative prowess of women and wives is often referred
to in epitaphs:

> Beneath this silent stone is laid,
> A noisy, antiquated maid.
> Who from her cradle talked till death,
> And ne'er before was out of breath.

But perhaps a man may, on this occasion, have the last word:

> This spot is the sweetest I've seen in my life,
> For it raises my flowers and covers my wife.

5. UNUSUAL DEATHS

It must be remembered that right down the years to the
latter part of last century life in most places except the biggest
towns was a very quiet, slow and probably monotonous exist-
ence, whose routine varied little from year to year. Hence any
event which interrupted this routine gained far more attention
then than it would do now. Death was the common lot to
which all would eventually come; but when death came
suddenly, by epidemic, accident or tragedy, the circumstances
were often sufficiently unusual to justify a special reference
in an epitaph.

Malmesbury is a small country town in north Wiltshire, and
in the graveyard of its lovely abbey is a headstone to Hannah
Twynnoy, who died on 23rd October 1703 after being attacked
by a wild animal which had escaped from a travelling circus
(plate 12):

> In bloom of Life
> She's snatch'd from hence,
> She had not room
> To make defence;
> For Tyger fierce
> Took Life away,
> And here she lies
> In a bed of Clay
> Until the Resurrection Day.

Celebration of 5th November is not by any means a recent
innovation. A headstone at **Minster-in-Sheppey**, Kent (plate
8), records the death of one Simon Gilker, Junior, aged 48
years, who 'was killed by means of a Rockett November 5th

15

1696'. In the case of a boy, Henry George Brown, who died on 20th March 1861, aged 10 years and 10 months, one wonders just what sort of structure is referred to (plate 18):

> How soon I was cut down. When innocent at play,
> The wind it blew a scaffold down and took my life
> away.

Tragedy in a small village could have a shattering effect on the local population. A modern mining disaster can affect a whole nation; early mining disasters were unhappily all too frequent and when they occurred they were often recorded in some detail in the epitaphs to the persons killed. An example of this comes from **Little Dean,** in the Forest of Dean, Gloucestershire, which also shows something of working hazards in 1819:

> These four youths were suddenly called into eternity on Tuesday the 6th day of April 1819 by an awful dispensation of the Almighty. The link of a chain employed to lower them into Bilston Pit breaking they were precipitated to the bottom of the Pit. Their bones literally dashed to pieces their bodies thus presenting a frightful and appalling spectacal to all who beheld them. They were interred in one grave on the Friday following being Good Friday April 9 1819. A Funeral Sermon was preached on the mournful occasion on Sunday April 25 1819. In the Church of Little Deane before a congregation of 2500 people on the following text which it was judged advisable to record upon their Tomb stone as a suitable admonition for the benefit of all survivors.
> Luke XIII vs 1, 2, & 3.
> Swift flew the appointed messenger of death and in a moment stopt their mortal breath. Art THOU prepared as suddenly to die? Tis mercy's call O list unto the cry.

Thomas Morgan	Aged 26
William Tingle	Aged 19
Robert Tingle	Aged 16
James Meredith	Aged 12

At **Normanton** churchyard, Leicestershire, appears this rather enigmatic verse:

> He died! how startling was his sudden fall
> He's gone obedient to th'Almighty's call;
> Dropt in a moment insensible of fear
> No thought disturb'd Him, no mistrust was near.

From **Old Dalby,** in the same county, is the even more infuriating epitaph on a slate headstone:

> 1835 Henry Wells who was killed.

To be deprived of the details is almost an affront to the reader of epitaphs who expects to be given too much rather than too little.

Deaths by drowning

Deaths caused by drowning are remarkably common, even in areas far removed from the coast. Many of these tragedies involved adults as well as children drowned in ponds and quite shallow streams. This is yet another reminder of the changing social scene in that the ability to swim only became common a little more than a century ago, when cheap railway travel brought seaside holidays and sea bathing within the reach of thousands of working-class people. Long before them, and typical of a rural drowning, the Cotswold village of **Barnsley,** near Cirencester, records the death of a 35-year-old man:

> O! Death, how sudden was thy stroke,
> The nearest Union Thou has broke;
> Nor gave me time to take my leave,
> Of my dear Parents left to grieve;
> The watery wave; which stop'd my breath,
> For want of help, soon caus'd my death.

From Edinburgh comes this inscription:

> Erected to the Memory of
>
> ———————
>
> John McFarlane
> Drown'd in the Water of Leith
>
> ———————
>
> By a few affectionate friends

From **Great Yarmouth** these lines commemorate Nicholas Round, drowned at sea:

> Here lies the body of Nicholas Round
> Who was lost in the sea and never was found.

Similarly from **Whitby:**

> Sudden and unexpected was the end
> Of our esteemed and beloved friend;
> He gave to all his friends a sudden shock
> By one day falling into Sunderland dock.

A young boy from **Betchworth,** Reigate, had an accident on ice:

> Dear Friends and companions all
> Pray warning take by me;
> Don't venture on the ice too far,
> As 'Twas the death of me.

A very well-restored stone (plate 15) in the churchyard at
Bosham, Sussex, has a carved relief of a ship on it, and
commemorates the master of the sloop *Two Brothers,* Thomas
Barrow, who 'by the Breaking of the Horse fell into the Sea
and was Drowned. October the 13th 1759, Aged 23 Years'.
Then follows a verse, some of whose lines occur, with slight
variations, in coastal churchyards all around our shores:

> Tho' Boreas's Storms and Neptune's waves have
> tos'd me to and fro
> Yet I at length by God's decree am harboured here
> below
> Where at an Anchor here I lay with many of our
> Fleet
> Yet once again I shall set Sail My Saviour Christ
> to meet.

The sinking of wells for water supply, or shafts in connection
with the driving of tunnels or working of mines, resulted in
many accidental deaths. Epitaphs to the victims of such
disasters often carried warnings or advice. At **Marton,** Yorkshire, in 1812, three men died 'by Venturing into a Well at
Marton when it was filled by Carbonic Acid gas, or fixed air.
From this unhappy accident let others take warning, not to
Venture in Wells Without first trying whether a Candle will
burn in them. If the candle burns to the bottom they may
be entered with safety; if it goes out, human life cannot be
supported'.

Deaths by fire and lightning

In 1781 at **Stoke Newington,** London, Elizabeth Picket was
burned to death when her clothing caught fire. Her gravestone
advises: 'Reader—if ever you should witness such an affecting
scene; recollect that the only method to extinguish the flame
is to stifle it by an immediate covering'. As it was quite a
usual rural practice for people—particularly elderly people—
to have fires in their bedrooms, with windows tightly closed,
this advice may not have been altogether out of place.

Lightning has been the cause of numerous deaths and such
sudden tragedies have obviously had a marked effect on rural
communities, for epitaphs to the deceased are often extremely
long and detailed. The village of **Stanton Harcourt,** Oxfordshire,
has a tombstone now set on the church wall, bearing verses
said to have been written by Alexander Pope for the Lord
Harcourt who paid for the stone (plate 17):

> Near this place lie the bodies of John Hewet and
> Sarah Drew, an industrious young man and virtuous
> maiden of this parish Contracted in Marriage who

18

being with many others at Harvest work were both in one instant killed by lightning on the last day of July 1718

> Think not by rigorous judgment seiz'd
> A pair so faithful could expire
> Victims so pure Heav'n saw well pleas'd
> And snatch'd them in celestial fire
> Live well and fear no sudden fate
> When God calls virtue to the grave
> Alike 'tis Justice soon or late
> Mercy alike to kill or save
> Virtue Unmov'd can hear the Call
> And face the flash that melts the Ball.

A similar, if moralising inscription, at **Bury St. Edmunds,** Suffolk, commemorates the death by lightning of a much younger girl:

> Here lies interred the Body of Mary Haselton, a young maiden of this town, born of Roman Catholic parents, and virtuously brought up, who, being in the act of prayer repeating her vespers, was instantaneously killed by a flash of lightning, August 16th 1785. Aged 9 years.

Twelve lines of verse follow, amplifying the moral of the unhappy event. Indeed, almost any event out of the ordinary gave an opportunity for a moralising tone to be adopted in the epitaph to the person who died as a result of it. **Bury St. Edmunds** has another example, near the previous one:

> Reader pause at this Humble Stone: it Records the fall of unguarded Youth, By the allurements of vice and the treacherous snares of Seduction. SARAH LLOYD, on the 25h of April 1800 in the 22d year of her Age. Suffer'd a Just but Ignominious Death for admitting her abandoned seducer into the Dwelling House of her Mistress, in the night of 3d Oct: 1799, and becoming the Instrument in his Hands of the crimes of Robbery and House-burning. These were her last Words: May my example be a Warning to Thousands.

A similarly awful but more public warning occurs not in a churchyard epitaph, but inscribed on the market cross of 1814, at **Devizes,** Wiltshire, where the mayor and corporation recorded that:

> On Thursday, the 25th January 1753, Ruth Pierce, of Potterne in this county, agreed with three other women to buy a sack of wheat in the market, each

paying her due proportion towards the same. One of these women, in collecting tne several quarters of money discovered a deficiency, and demanded of Ruth Pierce the sum which was wanting to make good the amount. Ruth Pierce protested that she had paid her share, and said that she wished she might drop dead if she had not. She rashly repeated this awful wish, when, to the consternation of the surrounding multitude, she instantly fell down and expired, having the money concealed in her hand.

Murder victims

A ledger stone at **Gilling,** near Richmond, Yorkshire, records the death in 1753 of a local youth in melodramatic circumstances (some of the words are almost indecipherable now):

Unto the mournful fate of young John Moore,
Who fell a victim to some villain's power;
In Richmond Lane, near to Aske Hall tis said,
There was his life most cruelly betray'd.
Shot with a gun by some abandon'd rake,
Then knock'd out with a hedging stake,
His soul, I trust, is with the blest above,
There to enjoy eternal rest and love;
Then let us pray his murderer to discover,
That he to justice may be brought over.

At **Wolstanton,** Staffordshire, the inscription to Sarah Smith (1763), free from libel laws, virtually identifies her murderer:

It was C. . . . . .s B. . . . . w
That brought me to my end
Dear parents, mourn not for me
For God will stand my friend.
With half a pint of Poyson
He came to visit me
Write this on my Grave
That all who read may see.

Another murder is recorded at St. Michael's, **Workington:**

Joseph Glendowing 1808
Murdered near this town June 15, 1808
His murderers were never discovered.
You villains! if this stone you see
Remember that you murdered me!
You bruised my head and pierced my heart
Also my bowels did suffer part.

Another from **Alnwick,** Northumberland:

> Here lieth Martin Elphinstone
> Who with his sword did cut in sunder
> The daughter of Sir Harry Crispe
> who did his daughter marry.
>
> She was fat and fulsome,
> But men will sometimes
> Eat bacon with their beans
> And love the fat as well as lean.

Now work that one out!

A soldier's murder is commemorated with military exactness and brevity at **Weeley,** Essex:

> Alexander M. Donald. Late soldier in the first battalion 79th regt. who in the prime of life was inumanly murdered near Little Clacton on the morning of the 26th July 1806. (This stone was renovated by the Queen's Own Cameron Highlanders.)

One of the most famous and unusual deaths of which details are recorded on the tombstone is also of a soldier, buried in the graveyard of **Winchester** cathedral, Hants.

> In Memory of THOMAS THETCHER a Grenadier in the North Regt. of Hants Militia, who died of a violent Fever contracted by drinking Small Beer when hot the 12th of May 1764. Aged 26 years. In grateful remembrance of whose universal goodwill towards his Comrades, this Stone is placed here at their expence, as a small testimony of their regard and concern.
>
> Here sleeps in peace a Hampshire Grenadier,
> Who caught his death by drinking cold small Beer,
> Soldiers be wise from his untimely fall
> And when ye're hot drink Strong or none at all.
>
> This memorial being decay'd was restor'd by the Officers of the Garrison A.D. 1781.
> An honest Soldier never is forgot
> Whether he die by Musket or by Pot.
> This Stone was replaced by the North Hants Militia when disembodied at Winchester on 26th April 1802, in consequence of the original Stone being destroyed.
>
> And again replaced by The Royal Hampshire Regiment 1966.

It may be wondered who was responsible for the verses and inscriptions recorded on tombstones from the seventeenth to the nineteenth centuries. Although the poets Pope, Gay, and Young were the most frequently quoted ones, most of the epitaphs were the work of local rhymesters, amateur poets such as schoolmasters, parsons and parish clerks, and some of this work would most likely have come from the ballads which were the stock-in-trade of pedlars. Certainly however the local parson was the best-educated and best-suited person to provide an appropriate epitaph for one of his parishioners who had died. One of the best of such local rural parsons was Canon Bowles, vicar of **Bremhill**, near Calne, Wilts., from 1805 to 1845. Many graves in the district have epitaphs written by him and he went so far as to have small books of verse printed which he then distributed free to his parishioners. One such example of his verse commemorates a soldier from Bremhill:

> A poor old soldier shall not lie unknown,
> Without a verse and this recording stone.
> 'Twas his, in youth, o'er distant lands to stray,
> Danger and death companions of his way.
> Here, in his native village, stealing age
> Closed the lone evening of his pilgrimage.
> Speak of the past—of names of high renown,
> Or brave commanders long to dust gone down,
> His look with instant animation glowed,
> Tho' ninety winters on his head had snow'd.
> His country, while he lived, a boon supplied,
> And Faith her shield held o'er him when he died.

Not great poetry perhaps, but appropriate, appealing and capable of being understood by villagers who read it. If the purpose of an epitaph was to perpetuate the memory of the departed, then a great many writers of such epitaphs succeeded very well. Virtues and faults may all have been recorded; cheerfulness would sometimes creep in, together with humour, and happily for us today, trades and professions were also often referred to.

Actors

Samuel Butler, actor, in St. Mary's, **Beverley**, Yorkshire:

> In Memory of SAMUEL BUTLER, A poor player that struts and frets his hour upon the stage, and then is heard no more. June 15th 1812. Aged 62.

David Garrick, the actor is commemorated by these lines in
Westminster Abbey:

> To paint fair nature, by divine command—
> Her magic pencil in his glowing hand—
> A Shakespeare rose—then to expand his fame
> Wide o'er this 'breathing world', a Garrick came.
> Though sunk in death the forms the poet drew,
> The actor's genius bade them breathe anew;
> Though, like the Bard himself, in night they lay,
> Immortal Garrick call'd them back to-day:
> And, till Eternity, with power sublime,
> Shall mark the mortal hour of hoary time,
> Shakespeare and Garrick like twin stars shall shine,
> And earth irradiate with beams divine.

And Garrick wrote these lines in **Bath Abbey,** to a fellow-actor,
James Quin:

> That tongue, which set the table in a roar,
> And charmed the public ear, is heard no more;
> Closed are those eyes, the harbingers of wit,
> Which spoke, before the tongue, what Shakespeare
> writ;
> Cold are those hands, which, living, were stretched
> **forth,**
> At friendship's call, to succour modest worth.
> Here is James Quin! Deign, reader, to be taught,
> Whate'er thy strength of body, force of thought,
> In Nature's happiest mould however cast,
> To this complexion thou must come at last.

At St. Peter Mancroft, **Norwich,** are epitaphs to two actresses.
To Anne Roberts who died in 1743 aged 30:

> The World's a Stage, at Birth our Plays begun,
> And all find Exits when their Parts are done.

And to Henrietta Bray (1737):

> Here, Reader, you may plainly see,
> That Wit nor Humour here could be
> A Proof against mortality.

Several actors and actresses of Norwich, who were famous in
the early eighteenth century, are similarly commemorated in
the district. In appropriate, and even briefer vein is the epitaph
to the great tragedian Richard Burbidge:

> Exit—Burbidge.

Equally brief, and even more famous, are the words to Shakespeare's famous contemporary, commemorated in Poets' Corner,
Westminster Abbey:

> O Rare Ben Jonson. Born 1574 at Westminster.
> Died 1637.

The famous clown, Grimaldi, simply has as his epitaph: 'Here am I'.

A well-known fool Dicky Pearce (1728), who had entertained noblemen and kings, is commemorated in the words of Jonathan Swift:

> Here lies the Earl of Suffolk's Fool,
> Men called him Dicky Pearce;
> His folly served to make men laugh,
> When wit and mirth were scarce.
> Poor Dick, alas! is dead and gone,
> What signifies to cry?
> Dicky's enough are still behind
> To laugh at by and by.

Anglers

In the graveyard of **Ripon** cathedral, Yorkshire, is this head-stone (plate 7):

> Here lies poor, but honest Bryan Tunstall; he was a most expert angler, until Death, envious of his Merit, threw out his line, hook'd him, and landed him here the 21st day of April 1790.

Architects

Sarnesfield, near Weobley, Herefordshire, has in the church-yard an unusal epitaph to John Abel (1577 - 1674). He built the now vanished market houses at Brecon, Kington and Leominster, and in 1645 constructed a powder-mill during the siege of Hereford, for which Charles I granted him the title of King's Carpenter. His stone shows three figures kneeling— Abel and his two wives, together with the tools of his trade, rule, compasses and set-square, and these lines:

> This craggy stone a covering is for an architector's bed;
> That lofty building raised high, yet now lies low his head;
> His line and rule, so death concludes, are locked up in store;
> Build then who list,
> Or they who wist,
> For he can build no more.
> His house of clay could hold no longer,
> May Heaven's joy build him a stronger. JOHN ABEL.

Colton, Staffordshire, has a memorial to James Heywood, who died in 1804, also showing the tools of his trade, with this verse:

> The Corner Stone I often times have dress'd,
> In Christ, the corner-stone, I now find rest;
> Though by the Builder he rejected were,
> He is my God, my Rock, I build on here.

An earlier epitaph from **Chobham**, Surrey, has a very pleasant metre and is to John Alexander, who died in 1757:

> Houses he built, with Brick, with Wood and stone;
> But all his art could not support his own;
> Death push'd, he strove, vain was ye weak essay;
> Down dropt at last his tenement of clay;
> Flatt as himself his houses time will throw;
> That JOHN e'er lived what mortal then will know;
> Yes, or one fabric he consigned to fame;
> The lasting fabric of an honest name.

Blacksmiths

William Andrews published a book in 1883 called *Curious Epitaphs*. Many rural occupations are mentioned in it, but a number of these examples have vanished. However the lines supposed to have been written by the poet Hayley occur in a number of churchyards, showing only very slight variations on the same theme:

> My sledge and hammer lie reclined,
> My bellows, too, have lost their wind;
> My fire's extinct, my forge decayed,
> And in the dust my vice is laid.
> My coal is spent, my iron's gone,
> My nails are drove, my work is done;
> My fire-dried corpse lies here at rest,
> And smoke-like, soars up to be bless'd.

Old Malton, Rochdale, Feltham, Bothwell, and **Westham** churchyards each are said to have stones bearing these words.

Carpenters

The tombstones of carpenters frequently show the tools of their trade. Mark Sharp's stone at St. John sub Castro, **Lewes,** Sussex, is a particularly good example and shows a saw, a plane, augers, mallet, axe, gouges, square, bevel, and compasses (plate 19); **Hanslope,** Buckinghamshire, commemorates Joseph Cox, senior, aged 92, and depicts the arms of the Carpenters' Company, as well as tools of the trade. The same stone also refers to his wife who died in 1762 (three years after her husband) aged 101, and the inscription continues 'their descendants at their death were 10 children 62 Grandchildren and 102 Great Grandchildren, in all 174'. **Ockham** churchyard, Woking, Surrey, commemorates John Spong, carpenter:

> Who many a sturdy oak had laid along,
> Fell'd by Death's surer hatchet here lies Spong.
> Posts oft he made, yet ne'er a place could get,
> And lived by railing, though he was no wit;
> Old saws he had, although no antiquarian,
> And stiles corrected, yet was no grammarian.

Clockmakers

Perhaps the finest example of any 'trade' tombstone in the country comes from **Lydford**, Devon, a few miles from Oke-hampton, where a chest-tomb bears on its upper surface this extraordinary inscription:

> Here lies, in horizontal position the outside case of GEORGE ROUTLEIGH, Watchmaker; Whose abilities in that line Were an honour to his profession, Integrity was the Mainspring, and prudence the Regulator, of all the actions of his life. Humane, generous and liberal, his hands never stopped till he had relieved distress. So nicely regulated were all his motions, that he never went wrong, except when set a-going by people who did not know his Key; even then he was easily set right again. He had the art of disposing his time so well, that his hours glided away in one continual round of pleasure and delight, Until an unlucky minute put a period to his existence. He departed this life Nov. 14, 1802: aged 57; wound up, In hopes of being taken in hand by his Maker; And of being thoroughly cleaned, repaired and set a-going in the world to come.

Berkeley, Gloucestershire, has a memorial to Thomas Peirce, who died in 1665, aged 77 (plate 11):

> Here Lyeth Thomas Peirce, whom no man taught
> Yet he in Iron, Brasse, and Silver wrought
> He Jacks, and Clocks, and watches (with Art) made
> And mended too when others worke did fade
> Of Berkeley five tymes Mayor this Artist was
> And yet this Mayor, this Artist was but Grasse
> When his own watch was downe on the last Day
> He that made watches had not made A Key
> To winde it Up, but Useless it must lie
> Untill he Rise Again no more to die.

Cricketers

In Hampshire, appropriately, is one of the few verses which commemorate a cricketer, John Small, in **Petersfield** churchyard (1826):

> Here lies, bowled out by Death's unerring ball . . .
> . . . this last of Hambledonians, old John Small,
> Gave up his bat and ball,
> His leather, wax, and all.

The memorial to Charles Sheldrick (1875) at **Sawston,** Cambridgeshire, shows a carving of cricket bat, ball, stumps, and pads; **Lewknor,** Oxfordshire, records that Thomas Smith died suddenly in 1885, and the memorial depicts in a small lunette a cricket ball breaking the wicket. A similar design is also on Richard Barlow's memorial at **Blackpool,** with the words 'Bowled at Last' and it can also be seen on the great Lillywhite's grave at **Highgate.**

Doctors

All the most desirable of a doctor's qualities seem to have been possessed by this country doctor at **Farleigh Hungerford,** near Bath, Somerset, whose epitaph reads:

> Sacred to the memory of Edward Fryer M.D. whose professional science, extensive knowledge, classical taste and profound judgement rendered his society the delight of the learned and the great. Physician to H.R.H. the Duke of Sussex he received honourable testimonies of confidence and esteem and for urbanity integrity and benevolence. He lived uniformly revered and died sincerely lamented. 1826.

Farmers

Verse epitaphs to farmers are rare; headstones showing carvings of agricultural implements are much more common, especially in particular localities. Around **Beaconsfield** and **Upton,** Buckinghamshire, and **Winkfield,** Berkshire, are a number of examples from the 1770s and 1780s, showing designs with ploughs, harrows, sickles, hay-forks, reaping-hooks, and rakes, grouped around a central sheaf. Other examples occur in **Kent,** at **Beckenham, Frindsbury** and **Sutton-at-Hone;** in Sussex, at **Sidlesham** and **Westbourne;** and in Gloucestershire at **Pebworth, Hardwicke,** and **Standish.** A modern stone at **Basildon,** Berkshire, commemorates Jethro Tull, 'Pioneer of Mechanized Agriculture . . . 1674-1740'.

Gamekeepers

Memorials to gamekeepers have occasionally produced some quite worthwhile epitaphs. An example from Worcestershire is in **Shrawley** churchyard, where a delicately carved relief shows the deceased firing his gun at a covey. This, and the epitaph accompanying it, is decaying sadly, but sufficient of the verse is left to enjoy:

> He sleeps! No more at early Morn
> To wake the Woods with mellow Horn;
> No more with willing Dog and Gun,
> To rise before the laggard Sun;
> No more before the social Can,
> To-morrow's sport with joy to Plan;
> Death took his aim, discharged his Piece,
> And bade his sporting Season cease.

An even more impressive example from Kells churchyard, **New Galloway,** in Kirkcudbrightshire, Scotland, shows a beautifully carved stone showing in relief the symbols of a sportsman's life—gun, powder-flask, fishing-rod, a grouse and a pointer dog (plate 13) with a verse on the opposite side of the headstone which won for its composer, the local minister, a prize of one guinea offered at the time for the best epitaph to the deceased gamekeeper, John Murray, who died in 1777:

> Ah John, what changes since I saw thee last;
> Thy fishing and thy shooting days are past.
> Bagpipes and hautboys thou canst sound no more;
> Thy nods, grimaces, winks, and pranks are o'er.
> Thy harmless, queerish, incoherent talk,
> Thy wild vivacity, and trudging walk
> Will soon be quite forgot. Thy joys on earth—
> A snuff, a glass, riddles, and noisy mirth—
> Are vanished all. Yet blest, I hope, thou art,
> For, in thy station, weel thou play'dst thy part.

Gardeners

Also in Kirkcudbrightshire, by the ruined Girthon church, near **Gatehouse of Fleet,** is the headstone to Robert Glover, gardener to the Cally Estate, who died in 1779 (plate 3). The homely symbols of his trade are carved on it in low relief—spade, hoe, and rake. In **Lambeth** churchyard, London, the Tradescant tomb of 1662 (repaired in 1773) commemorates the three famous Johns:

> '. . . gardeners to the Rose and Lily Queen . . . who
>   thence shall rise
> And change this Garden for a Paradise'.

Innkeepers

From **Great Bedwyn,** Wiltshire, but not in the churchyard, comes this memorial to an innkeeper:

> Beneath this stone in hopes of Zion,
> Doth lie the landlord of the Lion;
> His son keeps on the business still,
> Resigned upon the heavenly will.

It is fixed to the wall of the local monumental masons, bordering the main street through the village, in company with many others, from the eighteenth century onwards. Some of them have been re-lettered and painted in their original form so that the whole display represents a trade-sign en masse which is probably unique. The masons of this family have pursued the trade for two centuries and still do, and the village churchyard has many examples of their fine craftsmanship. The same epitaph to an innkeeper also occurs in the churchyard of **Upton-upon-Severn,** Worcestershire, but perhaps the best of all innkeepers' epitaphs, dated 1766, is from **Belbroughton,** Worcestershire. The upper part of the stone has a relief carving showing punchbowl, bottles, and pots, and commemorates Richard Philpots, keeper of the Bell inn:

> To tell a merry or a wondrous tale
> Over a cheerful glass of nappy ale,
> In harmless mirth was his supreme delight,
> To please his guests or friends by day or night.
> But no fine tale, how well soever told,
> Could make the tyrant, Death, his stroke withhold,
> That fatal stroke had laid him here in dust,
> To rise again once more with joy we trust.

Musicians

These lines commemorate an organ-blower from Wales:

> Under this stone lies Meredith Morgan,
> Who blew the bellows of our church organ,
> Tobacco he hated, to smoke most unwilling,
> Yet never so pleased as when pipes he was filling.
> No reflection on him for rude speech could be cast,
> Though he made our loud organ give many a blast.
> No puffer was he, though, a capital blower,
> He could fill double G, and now lies a note lower.

Musicians are commemorated in many churchyards, but usually with carvings showing their instruments, or even bars of music, rather than in the form of epitaphs. **Frampton-on-Severn,** Gloucestershire, has a memorial to William Keyes, a blacksmith, who died in 1795, and whose stone shows music-albums, violin and bow, flageolet, French horn and bassoon. The carving is probably the work of John Pearce, who was responsible for a tablet in **Westbury** church to Thomas Sinderby, who died in 1812, showing a violin and music-albums. Violins also occur on tombstones at **Spalding**, Lincolnshire, and **North Stoneham**, Hampshire, while at **Old Weston**, Huntingdonshire, a violinist is shown in the contemporary dress of 1809. Lyres and harps are common and, in terms of musical scores, the opening bars of 'I know that my Redeemer liveth' from *Messiah* seem to be favourites, being engraved on tombstones at **Burton Overy**, Leicestershire (1817), and at **Burbage** in the same county to William Garner (1881), organist at the parish church for 24 years. **Highgate** (London) has a grand piano carved on a tombstone, while **Hampstead** has a model pipe-organ, as has **Kildwick**, Yorkshire.

Parish clerks

These were important people in small rural communities, and memorials to them sometimes pay well-deserved tributes to their service and give an indication of the wide range of activities their service embraced. **Bakewell**, Derbyshire, commemorates two parish clerks, father and son—Samuel Row, died 1792, and Philip, died 1815:

> who now with Hallelujahs Sound
> Like Him can make the Roof rebound.

The father was not only parish clerk, but also sexton, singing-master, schoolmaster, and will-maker. At **Crayford**, Kent, Peter Isnell was clerk for thirty years:

> And here, with three wives, he awaits till again,
> The Trumpet shall arouse him to sing out Amen.

Bingham, Nottinghamshire, has a memorial to Thomas Hart, parish clerk for 58 years, and his epitaph has the lines:

> . . . correct he read and sung so well;
> His words distinct, his verse so clear . . .
> Death cut the brittle thread, and then,
> A period put to his Amen.

Poachers

Poachers seem to have been regarded with some degree of affection, and are commemorated quite frequently, especially in the Midlands. One of the best examples of a verse epitaph is that to a famous deer-poacher, who died in 1752, and was buried at **Nottingham:**

> Here lies a Marksman who with Art and Skill
> When Young and Strong the Bucks and Does did Kill,

Now Conquer'd by Grim Death (go Reader tell it)
He's now took leave of Powder, Gun and Pellett
A Fatal Dart which in the dark did fly
Has drop't him down amongst the dead to lie
If any want to know the poor slave's Name
T'was old Tom Booth ne'er ask from whence he came.

Policemen

Montgomery has a memorial stone to a policeman, William Davies, who died in 1903, showing a carved relief of helmet, belt, truncheon, and bull's eye lantern, within a wreath.

Railway engineers

There are two really fine headstones in **Bromsgrove** churchyard, Worcestershire, to engineers or drivers on the Birmingham and Gloucester Railway, who died through the explosion of an engine boiler (plate 20). The local red sandstone is rather soft, and these two stones, which stand side by side, have been painted black, with the lettering picked out clearly in white, for preservation and to make them easier to appreciate. In addition to a splendid epitaph, composed 'by an unknown friend', each headstone has in an oval panel at the top a low relief carving of a railway locomotive of that time (1840), showing an unusual amount of accurate detail. The better of the epitaphs is to Thomas Scaife, 'Late Engineer of the Birmingham and Gloucester Railway, who lost his life at Bromsgrove Station, by the Explosion of an Engine Boiler on Tuesday the 10 of November 1840':

My engine now is cold and still
No water does my boiler fill
My coke affords its flames no more
My days of usefulness are o'er
My wheels deny their noted speed
No more my guiding hands they heed
My whistle too has lost its tone
Its shrill and thrilling sounds are gone
My valves are now thrown open wide
My flanges now refuse to guide
My clacks, also, though once so strong
Refuse to aid the busy throng
No more I feel each urging breath
My steam is now condensed in death
Life's railway's o'er, each station's past
In death I'm stopp'd and rest at last
Farewell dear friends and cease to weep
In Christ I'm safe, in Him I sleep.

31

St. Mark's, **Swindon,** was built around 1850 specifically to serve the needs of the railwaymen and their families who were employed at the GWR works there and its churchyard has a number of memorials to railwaymen who died naturally or lost their lives in accidents. While on the subject of railways it is worthwhile pointing out the unique memorial on the edge of **Otley** churchyard, Yorkshire, which is in the form of a miniature railway tunnel. It commemorates 54 workmen who lost their lives during the building of the nearby Bramhope Tunnel (1845-49) and was erected at the expense of the employers.

Road-makers

John Metcalfe—'Blind Jack Metcalfe'—of Knaresborough, Yorkshire, is buried in **Spofforth** churchyard a few miles away. He became blind at the age of four after smallpox, but quite undaunted by this handicap, he went on to live a normal, full and active life. He married, became a soldier and was present at Culloden. He was a fine swimmer, followed the hounds and was a good violinist, but he is remembered most as a builder of roads, in the routing of which his blindness was an asset rather than a liability. Before he died in 1810 at 93 he had built or repaired hundreds of miles of roads in Yorkshire, Lancashire, Derbyshire and Cheshire, together with some houses and bridges. His headstone bears a poem written by Lord Dundas, his great admirer:

> Here lies John Metcalfe, one whose infant sight
> Felt the dark pressure of an endless night:
> Yet such the fervour of his dauntless mind,
> His limbs full strung, his spirit unconfin'd,
> That, long ere yet life's bolder years began;
> The sightless efforts Mark'd th' aspiring man;
> Not mark'd in vain—high deeds his manhood dar'd
> And commerce, travel, both his ardour shar'd.
> 'Twas his a guide's unerring aid to lend;
> O'er trackless wastes to bid new roads extend;
> And when Rebellion rear'd her giant size,
> 'Twas his to burn with patriot enterprize;
> For parting wife and babes one pang to feel,
> Then welcome danger for his country's weal.
> Reader! like him, exert thy utmost talent giv'n
> Reader! like him, adore the bounteous hand of Heav'n.

1. One of the finest of the Cotswold bale tombs, at Shipton-under-Wychwood, to eighteenth-century members of the Morgan family.

2. A group of table tombs and pedestal tombs at Painswick, Gloucestershire.

3. The memorial to Robert Glover, a gardener, at Girthon, Gatehouse of Fleet, Kirkcudbrightshire.

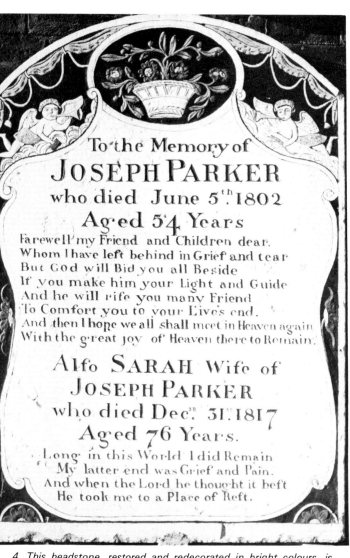

To the Memory of
JOSEPH PARKER
who died June 5th. 1802
Aged 54 Years

Farewell my Friend and Children dear.
Whom I have left behind in Grief and tear
But God will Bid you all Beside
If you make him your Light and Guide
And he will rife you many Friend
To Comfort you to your Lives end.
And then I hope we all shall meet in Heaven again
With the great joy of Heaven there to Remain.

Alfo **SARAH** Wife of
JOSEPH PARKER
who died Dec.r 31. 1817
Aged 76 Years.

Long in this World I did Remain
My latter end was Grief and Pain.
And when the Lord he thought it beft
He took me to a Place of Reft.

4. This headstone, restored and redecorated in bright colours, is outside a mason's workshop at Great Bedwyn, Wiltshire.

In Memory of
A generous, but unfortunate Sailor,
Who was barbarouſly murder'd on Hindhead,
On Sepʳ 24ᵗʰ 1786,
By three Villains,
After he had liberally treated them,
And promiſed them his farther Aſſiſtance,
On the Road to Portſmouth.

―――――

When pitying Eyes to ſee my Grave ſhall come,
And with a generous Tear bedew my Tomb;
Here ſhall they read my melancholy Fate,
With Murder and Barbarity complete.
In perfect Health, and in the Flow'r of Age,
I fell a Victim to three Ruffians Rage;
On bended Knees I mercy ſtrove t' obtain,
Their Thirſt of Blood made all Entreaties vain,
No dear Relation, or ſtill dearer Friend,
Weeps my hard Lot, or miſerable End;
Yet o'er my ſad Remains, (my Name unknown,)
A generous Public have inſcrib'd this Stone.

5. *The tombstone of a murdered sailor at Thursley, Surrey.*

SACRED
TO THE MEMORY OF
GEORGE H.J. BELOE,
THE BELOVED SON OF
LOUISA BELOE,
who was unfortunately drowned
by the fall
of the Suspension Bridge
THE 2ND OF MAY 1845,
AGED 9 YEARS.

FAREWELL DEAR BOY NO MORE I PRESS.
THY FORM OF LIGHT AND LOVELINESS.
AND THOSE WHO GAZED ON THY SWEET FACE
KNEW IT TO BE AN ANGLES DWELLING PLACE
AND IF THAT REALM WHERE THOU ART NOW
BE FILLED WITH BEINGS SUCH AS THOU
FROM SIN SET FREE AND SORROW FREED
THEN HEAVEN MUST BE A HEAVEN INDEED.

ALSO
MARGARET BE

6. *A tragic accident is recalled by this stone in the churchyard of St Nicholas, Great Yarmouth.*

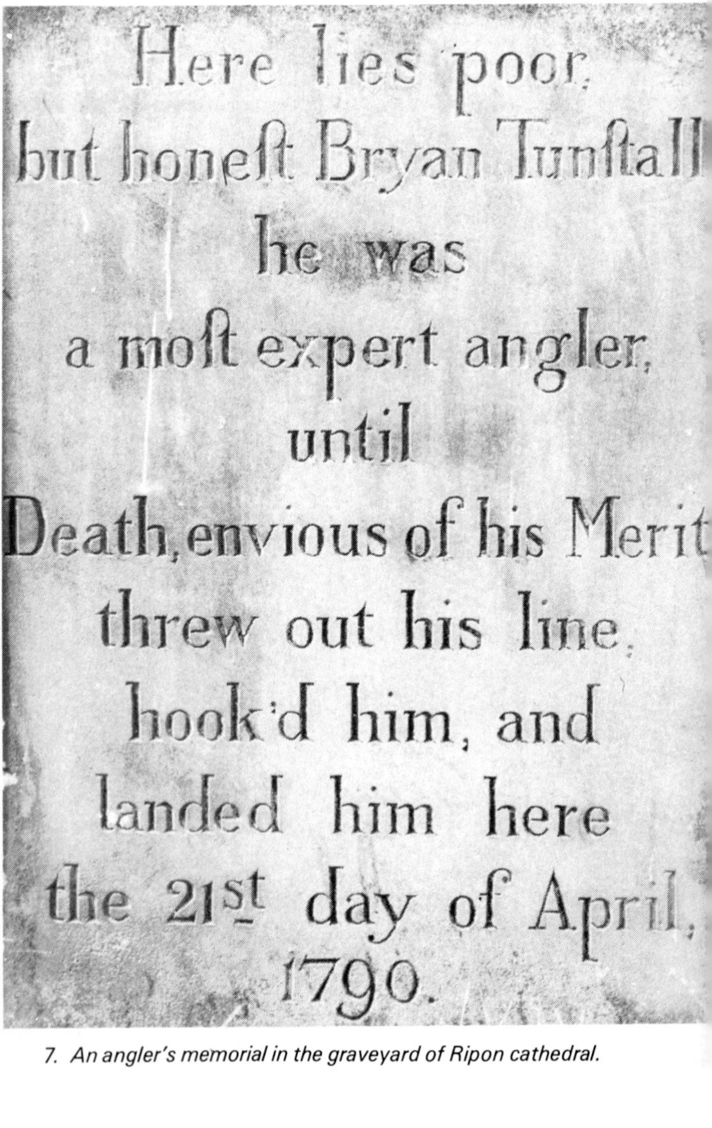

Here lies poor,
but honest Bryan Tunstall
he was
a moſt expert angler,
until
Death, envious of his Merit
threw out his line,
hook'd him, and
landed him here
the 21ˢᵗ day of April,
1790.

7. An angler's memorial in the graveyard of Ripon cathedral.

8. The gravestone of Simon Gilker at Minster-in-Sheppey, Kent. He was killed by a rocket on 5th November 1696.

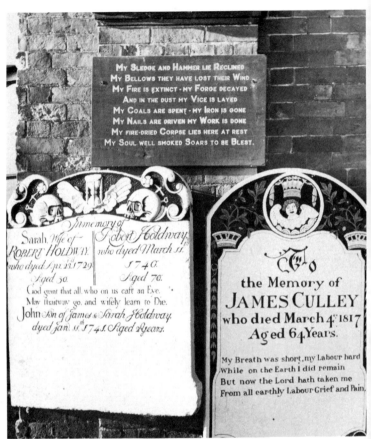

MY SLEDGE AND HAMMER LIE RECLINED
MY BELLOWS THEY HAVE LOST THEIR WIND
MY FIRE IS EXTINCT · MY FORGE DECAYED
AND IN THE DUST MY VICE IS LAYED
MY COALS ARE SPENT · MY IRON IS GONE
MY NAILS ARE DRIVEN MY WORK IS DONE
MY FIRE-DRIED CORPSE LIES HERE AT REST
MY SOUL WELL SMOKED SOARS TO BE BLEST.

In memory of
Sarah. Wife of   Robert Holdway,
ROBERT HOLDWAY,   who dyed March 11th
who dyed Apr. 23 1729   1740.
Aged 30.   Aged 70.
God grant that all. who on us cast an Eye.
May straitway go. and wisely learn to Die.
John Son of James & Sarah Holdway.
dyed Jan. 9th 1741. Aged 2 years.

To
the Memory of
JAMES CULLEY
who died March 4th 1817
Aged 64 Years.

My Breath was short, my Labour hard
While on the Earth I did remain
But now the Lord hath taken me
From all earthly Labour Grief and Pain,

9. *More memorial stones outside the mason's workshop at Great Bedwyn. The lower two came from the local churchyard.*

HERE LIE THE BODIES OF

JACOB WILLIAMS.   DAVID ROBERTS.
OWEN HUGHS.   THOMAS COLLINS.
CHARLES CAWLEY.   RICHARD CUTLER.
WILLIAM LOYD.   WILLIAM ELIOTT.
THOMAS BROWN.   JEMMY.
who were drifted on shore in a boat, frozen to death, at
Tregurrian Beach in this Parish, on Sunday 13th. D...

MDCCCXLVI.

10. *This memorial in St Mawgan churchyard, Cornwall, recalls a tragedy of 1846.*

11. *An interesting epitaph at Berkeley, Gloucestershire, to Thomas Peirce, a watchmaker.*

Here Lyeth Thomas peirce, whom no man taught
Yet he in Iron Brasse and Silver wrought
He Jacks, and Clocks, and Watches (with Art) made
And mended too when others worke did fade
Of Berkeley fiue tymes Major this Artist was
And Yet this Major, this Artist was but Grasse
When his owne Watch was Downe on the laſt Dā
He that made Watches, had not made A Key
To winde it Vp, but Vselesse it must lie
Vntill he Rise AGaine no more to die.

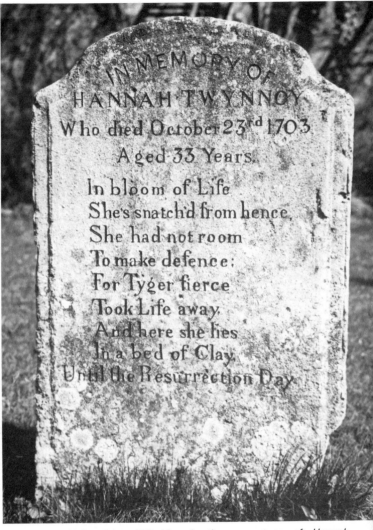

IN MEMORY OF
HANNAH TWYNNOY
Who died October 23ʳᵈ 1703
Aged 33 Years.

In bloom of Life
She's snatch'd from hence,
She had not room
To make defence;
For Tyger fierce
Took Life away,
And here she lies
In a bed of Clay,
Until the Resurrection Day.

12. At Malmesbury, Wiltshire, is the gravestone of Hannah
Twynnoy, who was killed by a tiger which had escaped from
a circus.

In memory of John Murray,
who died at Kenmore Jan 3 1777
aged 62 years, and who for 56
years, had been a faithfull servant to the family of Kenmore.

13. Grouse, gun-dog and the tools of his trade decorate the memorial of John Murray, a gamekeeper, at Kells, New Galloway, Scotland.

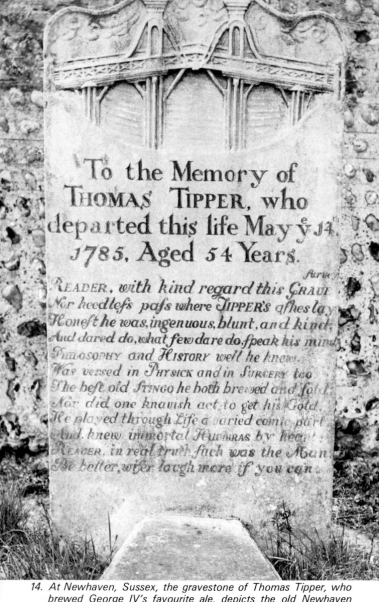

To the Memory of
THOMAS TIPPER, who
departed this life May y^e 14.
1785, Aged 54 Years.

READER, with kind regard this GRAVE survey
Nor heedless pass where TIPPER'S ashes lay
Honest he was, ingenuous, blunt, and kind;
And dared do, what few dare do, speak his mind,
PHILOSOPHY and HISTORY well he knew
Was versed in PHYSICK and in SURGERY too,
The best old STINGO he both brewed and sold,
Nor did one knavish act to get his Gold.
He played through Life a varied comic part,
And knew immortal HUDIBRAS by heart.
READER, in real truth such was the Man,
Be better, wiser, laugh more if you can.

14. At Newhaven, Sussex, the gravestone of Thomas Tipper, who
brewed George IV's favourite ale, depicts the old Newhaven
bridge.

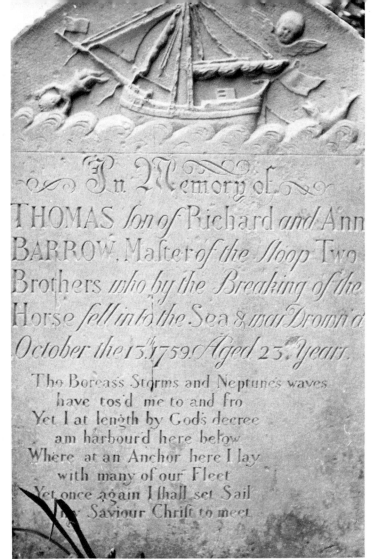

In Memory of
THOMAS *son of* Richard *and* Ann
BARROW, Master *of the* Sloop Two
Brothers *who by the Breaking of the*
Horse *fell into the* Sea & *was Drown'd*
October *the* 15th 1759 *Aged* 23 *Years*.

Tho Boreass Storms and Neptunes waves
have tos'd me to and fro
Yet I at length by Gods decree
am harbourd here below
Where at an Anchor here I lay
with many of our Fleet
Yet once again I shall set Sail
my Saviour Christ to meet

15. The memorial and epitaph to Thomas Barrow, a sailor, at Bosham, Sussex.

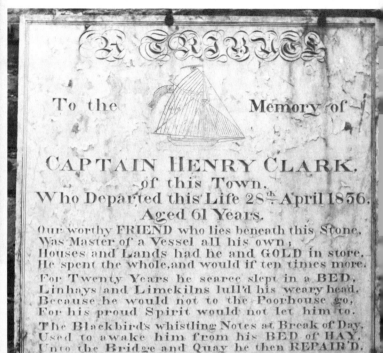

A TRIBUTE

To the   Memory of

CAPTAIN HENRY CLARK,
of this Town,
Who Departed this Life 28th April 1856,
Aged 61 Years.

Our worthy FRIEND who lies beneath this Stone,
Was Master of a Vessel all his own;
Houses and Lands had he and GOLD in store,
He spent the whole, and would if ten times more.

For Twenty Years he scarce slept in a BED,
Linhays and Limekilns lull'd his weary head,
Because he would not to the Poorhouse go,
For his proud Spirit would not let him to.

The Blackbird's whistling Notes at Break of Day,
Used to awake him from his BED of HAY,
Unto the Bridge and Quay he then REPAIR'D,
To see what SHIPPING up the River steer'd.

OFT in the week he used to VIEW the Bay,
To see what SHIPS were coming in from Sea,
To Captains wives he brought the welcome News,
And to the Relatives of all their CREWS.

At last poor HARRY CLARK was taken Ill,
And carried to the Workhouse 'gainst his Will,
But being of this mortal Life quite tired,
He liv'd about a Month and then expired

16. *Another mariner, Henry Clark, is commemorated by this epitaph at Bideford, Devon.*

NEAR THIS PLACE LIE THE BODIES OF

JOHN HEWET AND SARAH DREW

AN INDUSTRIOUS YOUNG MAN AND

VIRTUOUS MAIDEN OF THIS PARISH

CONTRACTED IN MARRIAGE

WHO BEING WITH MANY OTHERS AT HARVEST

WORK, WERE BOTH IN ONE INSTANT KILLED

BY LIGHTNING ON THE LAST DAY OF JULY

1718.

Think not by rigorous judgment seiz'd
A Pair so faithful could expire;
Victims so pure Heav'n saw well pleas'd
And snatch'd them in cœlestial fire.

Live well & fear no sudden fate
When God calls virtue to the grave
Alike 'tis Justice soon or late
Mercy alike to kill or save.

Virtue unmov'd can hear the Call
And face the Flash that melts the Ball.

17. Lord Harcourt, paid for this stone at Stanton Harcourt, Oxon, to be erected to two young farm workers who were killed by lightning. Alexander Pope is said to have written the verse.

18. The sad death of a boy at play is described on his wooden memorial at St Mary's, Baldock, Hertfordshire.

In Memory of HENRY GEORGE, Son of HENRY & HARRIET BROWN who Departed this LIFE MAR: 20 1861 Aged 10 YEARS & 10 MONTHS
How soon I was cut down. When innocent at play.
The wind it blew a scaffold down and took my LIFE away..

19. On the headstone of carpenter Mark Sharp at St John-sub-Castro, Lewes, Sussex, the tools of his trade are illustrated.

20. Two railwaymen's tombstones at Bromsgrove, Worcestershire.

SACRED
TO THE MEMORY OF THOMAS SCAIFE,
late an Engineer on the Birmingham and Gloucester Railway,
who lost his life at Bromsgrove Station, by the Explosion of
an Engine Boiler   Tuesday the 10 of November 1840.

He was 28 Years of Age highly esteemed by his fellow workmen
for his many amiable qualities, and his Death will be long lamented
by all those who had the pleasure of his acquaintance.

The following lines were composed by an unknown Friend
as a Memento of the worthiness of the Deceased.

My engine now is cold and still.   My flanges all refuse to guide.
No water does my boiler fill;   My clock also, though once so strong,
My coke affords its flame nomore.   Refuse to aid the busy throng.
My days of usefulness are o'er   No more I feel each working breath,
My wheels deny their noted speed   My steam is now condens'd in death.
Nomore my guiding hands they heed   Life's railway's o'er each station's past.
My whistle too, has lost its tone.   In death I'm stopp'd and rest at last.
Its shrill and thrilling sounds are gone.   Farewell dear friends and once lov'd mates
My valves are now thrown open wide.   In Christ I'm safe, in Him I sleep.

THIS STONE WAS ERECTED AT THE JOINT EXPENCE
OF HIS FELLOW WORKMEN 1842

PRATT Eng.

SACRED
TO THE MEMORY OF
JOSEPH   RUTHERFORD,
LATE ENGINEER TO THE BIRMINGHAM AND GLOUCESTER
RAILWAY,   COMPANY
who Died Nov 11 1840 Aged 32 Years.

Oh! Reader stay and cast an eye,
Upon this Grave wherein I lie .
For cruel Death has challenged me,
And soon alas, will call on thee ;
Repent in time, make no delay,
For Christ will call you all away.

My time was spent like day in sun,
Beyond all cure, my glass is run

Sailors

As is to be expected, sailors' tombstones are very common in coastal churchyards and nautical equipment inevitably forms a large part of the decorative carving which many of them bear. **Ramsgate** (St. Lawrence), Kent, has a stone of 1903 with this unusual inscription:

> This marks the wreck of Robert Woolward, who sailed the seas for fifty-five years. When Resurrection gun fires, the wreck will be raised by the Angelic Salvage Co: surveyed and if found worthy refitted, and started on the voyage to Eternity.

Scarborough has several memorials with anchors and rudders, and the **Portsmouth** area is particularly rich in sailors' graves. In the West Country the churchyards of **Appledore** and **Bideford,** Devon, have some splendid tombstones. This, on the church wall at Bideford, to a retired sea-captain, seems to portray exactly that type of character seen even today at little seaports, though Henry Clark, whom it commemorates, died in 1836 (plate 16):

> For twenty years he scarce slept in a bed;
> Linhays and limekilns lull'd his weary head
> Because he would not to the poor house go,
> For his proud spirit would not let him to.
>
> The black bird's whistling notes at break of day
> Used to awake him from his bed of hay.
> Unto the bridge and quay he then repaired
> To see what shipping up the river stirr'd.
>
> Oft in the week he used to view the bay,
> To see what ships were coming in from sea,
> To captain's wives he brought the welcome news,
> And to the relatives of all the crews.
>
> At last poor Harry Clark was taken ill,
> And carried to the workhouse 'gainst his will:
> And being of this mortal life quite tired,
> He lived about a month and then expired.

Servants

There are many memorials erected by masters to their servants, most of them from the days when it was commonplace for a servant to be in the employment of one family for all his working life. Indeed, a book of epitaphs was published in 1891 with the title *Faithful Servants,* and it included almost

700 examples of such epitaphs. Many of these refer to the peculiarly unique master-servant relationship and many head-stones to servants also include the master's name as well—quite often in larger letters! Some characteristic examples are given here; from **Edmondthorpe,** Leicestershire, a slate head-stone records:

> Here lieth the Body of Thomas Fanton who was Born at Warwick A.D. 1683. In 1693 he was hired by Ld Chief Baron Smith with whom he liv'd 14 years; He was then recommend'd (by Ld Ch Baron) to Sr Edwd Smith Bart in whose Service he continued till ye time of Sr Edwds death wch was 14 Years. He was then Servant to Edwd Smith Esq of this place wth wm he liv'd 35 Years who in remembrances of his many years Honest and Faithful Services order'd this stone to be Erected to his Memory. He died very justly Lamented by all who knew him.

Thus are remembered 63 years of service to one family. A much more humble epitaph at **Hillingdon,** Middlesex, com-memorates John and Mary Norton, who died in 1817 and 1850 respectively:

> Industrious servants we have been
> And some few troubles we have seen
> In this world we have done our best
> In hopes our souls are gone to rest.

Some eighteenth-century memorials to servants record negroes, probably earlier released from slavery by British travellers overseas. Best-known of these is the grave in **Henbury** church-yard, Bristol, to the 'running footman' of the Earl of Suffolk, whose death is said to have been the result of running from London:

> Here Lieth the body of SCIPIO AFRICANUS, Negro Servant of the Rt. Honourable Charles William, Earl of Suffolk and Bristol. Who died ye 21 Dec, 1720.

Shepherds

These were always highly regarded members of rural com-munities and are often commemorated in characteristic fashion. A slate headstone at **Burton Lazars,** Leicestershire, shows a splendidly cut engraving of a shepherd's crook with shears, as does **Hothfield,** Kent, while **Church Honeybourne,** Wor-cestershire, includes the shepherd and a sacrificial lamb, carved in relief by Hobday, but now badly eroded. **Miserden,** Gloucestershire, has this epitaph to a shepherd:

> To the memory of Samuel Horrell in this County
> a Shepherd who died aged 54 in 1807.
>
> From youth through life the sheep was all his care,
> And harmless as the flock his manners were.
> On earth he held the faith to Christians giv'n
> In hopes to join the fold of Christ in Heav'n.

Similar sentiments are expressed in another shepherd's memorial, not in a churchyard, but on the lower slopes of Skiddaw mountain, near **Keswick,** which commemorates three men of the Howell family, of nearby Lonscale, who were all shepherds in these open Lakeland hillsides:

> Great Shepherd of Thy heavenly flock
> These men have left our hill
> Their feet were on the living rock
> Oh guide and bless them still.

Shoemakers

Commemorated in County Durham, at **Seaham,** is Joseph Blackett, who died in 1810, and perhaps because he was also a poet his epitaph was written by Lord Byron. These are the lines on his tombstone:

> Stranger! behold interr'd together
> The souls of learning and of leather.
> Poor Joe is gone, but left his awl—
> You'll find his relics in a stall.
> His work was neat, and often found
> Well-stitched and with morocco bound.
> Tread lightly—where the bard is laid
> He cannot mend the shoe he made;
> Yet he is happy in his hole
> With verse immortal as his sole.
> But still to business he held fast
> And stuck to Phoebus to the last.
> Then who shall say so good a fellow
> Was only leather and prunella?
> For character—he did not lack it,
> and if he did—'twere shame to Black-it!

Soldiers

Soldiers' epitaphs have already been quoted, from Winchester and Bremhill (pages 21 and 22). However, a further famous example from **Minster-in-Sheppey,** Kent, to Henry Worth, a gunner, who died in 1779 and whose stone shows two cannon, reads thus:

> Deep in the earth his carcase lies entomb'd,
> Which Love and Grog for him had honeycomb'd,
> His match now burnt, expended all his priming,
> He left the World and us without ere whining,
> Jesting apart, Retired from wind and Weather,
> Virtue and WORTH are laid asleep together.

The hazards of military life were by no means confined to the battlefield, as this stone, thought to be at **Woolwich,** shows:

> Sacred to the memory of MAJOR JAMES BRUSH who was killed by the accidental discharge of a pistol by his orderly, 14th April 1831.
> 'Well done good and faithful servant'.

Wagoners

At **Palgrave,** Suffolk, is this epitaph to John Catchpole, accompanied by a carving of a wagon drawn by three pairs of horses and dated 1787:

> My horses have done Running, my Waggon is decay'd,
> And now in the Dust my Body is lay'd;
> My whip is worn out and my Work it is done,
> And now I'm broght here to my last home.

7. EPITAPHS TO THE FAMOUS

The playwright-composer John Gay is commemorated in **Westminster Abbey** by these lines:

> Life is a jest, and all things shew it;
> I thought so once, but now I know it.

To which the great poet, Alexander Pope, has added:

> Well, then poor Gay lies underground!
> So there's an end of honest Jack!
> So little justice here he found
> It's ten to one he'll ne'er come back.

Pope died in 1744 and is buried at **Twickenham.** For his own epitaph he wrote:

> For one who would not be buried at Westminster Abbey.

> Heroes and kings your distance keep,
> In peace let one poor poet sleep,
> Who never flattered folks like you,
> Let Horace blush and Virgil too.

John Donne, clergyman, religious writer, poet, an eloquent and witty preacher who was described by Dryden as the 'greatest wit, though not the poet, of our nation', is buried in **St. Paul's,** and his epitaph reads, simply:

> Reader, I am to let thee know,
> Donne's body only lies below;
> For could the grave his soul comprise,
> Earth would be richer than the skies.

Sir Walter Raleigh's memorial in St. Margaret's, **Westminster** (1618) bears these lines:

> Even such in time, which takes in trust
> Our youth and joyes and all we have,
> And payes us but with age and dust,
> Which in the dark and silent grave,
> When we have wandered all our wayes,
> Shuts up the story of our dayes,
> And from which earth, and grave, and dust,
> The Lord shall raise me up, I trust.

Admiral Blake, who died in 1657 while entering **Plymouth** Harbour after cruising off Cadiz, was originally buried in Westminster Abbey, but was later re-interred in St. Margaret's,

Westminster, and is commemorated in these lines:

> Here lies a man made Spain and Holland shake,
> Made France to tremble and the Turks to quake.
> Thus he tam'd men, but if a lady stood
> In's sight, it rais'd a palsy in his blood;
> Cupid's antagonist, who on his life
> Had fortune as familiar as a wife.
> A stiff, hard soldier; for he,
> It seems, had more of Mars than Mercury.
> At sea he thunder'd, calm'd each rising wave,
> And now he's dead, sent thundering to the grave.

Oliver Goldsmith's lines to the writer Edward Purdon, are often quoted:

> Here lies Ned Purdon, from misery freed,
> Who long was a bookseller's hack;
> He led such a damnable life in this world,
> I don't think he'll ever come back.

Charles and Mary Lamb are buried in the churchyard at All Saints, **Edmonton,** North London:

> To the Memory of Charles Lamb, Died 27th Decr.
> 1834, aged 59.
> Farewell dear friend, that smile, that harmless mirth
> No more shall gladden our domestic hearth;
> That rising tear, that pain forbid to flow,
> Better than words no more assuage our woe;
> That hand outstretched, from small but well earned
>   store,
> Yield succour to the destitute no more.
> Yet art thou not all lost; thro' may an age
> With sterling sense and humour shall thy page
> Win many an English bosom, pleased to see
> That old and happier vein revived in thee.
> This for our earth, and if with friends we share
> Our joys in Heaven, we hope to meet thee there.
> Also Mary Lamb, sister of the above,
> Born 3rd Decr. 1767, died 20th May 1847.

King Charles II asked the Earl of Rochester to compose an epitaph for him, with this result:

> Here lies our Sovereign Lord the King,
> Whose word no man relies on;
> Who never said a foolish thing,
> Nor ever did a wise one.

(One version has 'mutton-eating King' in the first line.)
It is reported that the King's comments on Rochester's lines

took the form of a suitable riposte:

> If death could speak, the King would say,
> In justice to his crown,
> His acts they were his ministers',
> His words they were his own.

8. MISCELLANY

One of the best known epitaphs typical of English eccentricity is at **Kingsbridge**, Devon, and shows that sense of humour which manages to break through the inevitability of death:

> Underneath Lieth the Body of Robert Comonly Called
> Bone Phillip who died July 27th 1793 Aged 63 Years
> At whose request the following lines are here inserted
>
> Here lie I at the Chancel door
> Here lie I because I'm poor
> The farther in the more you'll pay
> Here lie I as warm as they.

Puns

Puns are to be expected in an epitaph to a man called Knott, and from **Bromsgrove**, Worcestershire, comes this:

> Here lies a man that was Knott born,
> His father was Knott before him.
> He lived Knott, and did Knott die,
> Yet underneath this stone doth lie;
> Knott christened,
> Knott begot,
> And here he lies,
> And yet was Knott.

Similar word-play is recorded from Lincolnshire and **Esher** (Surrey) on stones each commemorating a John Miles:

> This tombstone is a Milestone:
> Ha! How so?
> Because beneath lies MILES,
> Who's Miles below.

A simple couplet from **Luton**:

> Here lies the body of Thomas Procter,
> Who lived and died without a doctor.

Dr. Potter, Archbishop of Canterbury, 1736, is neatly commemorated in this couplet:

> Alack and well a-day
> Potter himself is turned to clay.

Thomas Fuller, D.D., born 1608, died 1661, is remembered more briefly:

> Here lies Fuller's earth.

Sir Richard Worme, **Peterborough** cathedral:

> Does Worm eat Worme? Knight Worme this truth
> confirms,
> For here, with worms, lies Worme, a dish for worms.
> Does worm eat Worme? Sure Worme will this deny,
> For Worme with worms, a dish for worms don't lie.
> 'Tis so and 'tis not so, for free from worms,
> 'Tis certain Worme is blest without his worms.

Mrs. Stone, in **Melton Mowbray** churchyard:

> Curious enough, we all must say,
> That what was stone must now be clay;
> Most curious still, to own we must,
> That what was stone must soon be dust.

And from a **Liverpool** churchyard:

> Poor John lies buried here;
> Although he was both hale and stout,
> Death stretched him on the bitter bier,
> In another world he hops about.

Epigrams

From St. John's, **Devizes** and **Llandovery**:

> Life's uncertain — Death is sure
> Sin is the wound — Christ's the cure.

From **West Linton**, Howden, Yorkshire:

> Man's life's a vapour, full of woes
> He cuts a caper and off he goes.

Hammersmith, to one Jean Anderson, 1770, also at **North Mimms,** Hertfordshire, to James Goddard (1754):

> Praises on tombs are vainly spent,
> A good name is a monument.

From **Cirencester** churchyard, Gloucestershire:

> Death takes the good, too good on earth to stay
> And leaves the bad, too bad to take away.

From **Dorchester** Abbey, Oxfordshire, the miserliness of a man is recorded:

> Here lies one who for medicine would not give
> A little gold; and so his life he lost;
> I fancy that he'd wish again to live
> Did he but know how much his funeral cost.

Self-pitying, from **Saddleworth**, Yorkshire, is this lonely bachelor's lament:

> At three score winters' end I died,
> A cheerless being soul and sad,
> The nuptial knot I never tied,
> And wish my father never had.

A gentle scepticism of the waters of Bath is given in these lines on a tablet in **Bath** Abbey:

> These walls, adorned with monumental busts,
> Shew how Bath waters serve to lay the dust.

John Racket, from **Woodton**, Norfolk, has these lines on his tomb—the last three occurring in other places as well:

> Here lies John Racket
> In his wooden jacket,
> He kept neither horses nor mules;
> He lived like a hog,
> He died like a dog,
> And left all his money to fools.

A warning from Wales—in the church at **Llanfair Discoed:**

> Whoever here on Sunday
> Should practice playing at ball
> It may be before Monday
> The devil will have you all.

Less severe is this cautionary epitaph from a Dorset church:

> Man's Life.
> Man is a glass:
> Life is a water that's weakly
> Walled about:
> Sin bringes death:
> Death breaks the glass:
> So runnes the water out.
> Finis.

A pleasant mixture of metaphors comes from **Winchcombe**, Gloucestershire, but the first word is missing in this interesting epitaph of 1740:

> . . . death of all Men is the total Sum
> The period into which we all must come
> He lives but a short life who lives the longest
> And is weak in death in life was strongest
> Our life is like Cobwebs be we never so gay
> And Death the broom which sweeps us all away.

One of the briefest epitaphs still justifying the name appears on a stone at **Evesham,** Worcestershire:

> Here doth ly
> All that can dy
> Of Ann Haines who ended this life . . . May 1717.

At the other end of the scale is an example from **Wylye**
churchyard, Wiltshire, which may well have been written by
Thomas Dampier, who was parson there for 72 years, from
1759 to 1831.

> The Great, Vain Polish'd Marbles raise
> To those, who seldom merit Praise.
> But here the Widow and the Friend
> A man of Real Worth commend
> The Neighbour whose Calm Peaceful Life
> Gave no Disturbance, made no Strife:
> The Husband, the Relation Dear,
> The Christian Pious and Sincere.
> A Character so Far and True,
> None but the Virtuous will pursue.
> Who at the last Dread Trumpets Sound
> Shall rise and Be with Glory Crowned.

An unusual and often quoted verse is on a tombstone (1816)
at **Childrey,** Berkshire, but which is said to have been used
in other places, even as early as 1689.

> This world is wide
> And full of crooked streets
> Death is the market-place
> Where all men meet:
> If life was merchandise
> As men could buy
> The rich would live
> And the poor must die.

These lines may well have been part of the stock-in-trade
of a pattern-pedlar, confusing in thought because they come
from two different sources—the first half from an old and
well-known ballad *Death and the Lady,* the second half from
Wootton's *Remaines,* published in the sixteenth century. The
influence of old ballads right down into late Georgian times
is shown in this example from **Gilmorton,** Leicestershire, of
1750:

> Earth walks on Earth, like glittering Gold;
> Earth says to Earth, all's made of mould;
> Earth builds on Earth, Castle and Towers,
> Earth to Earth, all shall be Ours.

This quatrain is actually founded on some English lyrics of
the thirteenth century. Much simpler to understand is the

ragpickers' epitaph from **West Down,** Devon, 1797, **and Wymondham,** Leicestershire, 1809:

> Reader, pass on, nor waste your precious time
> On bad biography and murdered rhyme;
> What I was before's well known to my neighbours
> What I am now is no concern of yours.

Various metaphors are used for the grave. **Chipping Sodbury,** Gloucestershire, has a stone to Elizabeth Oldfield (1642), in which her grave is described as 'The Wardrobe of my dusty clothes'. Commonest comparison is as a bed or 'tenement of clay', as at **Finedon,** Northamptonshire:

> Here lyeth Richard Dent, in his last tenement.

Or at **Folkestone,** from 1688, come these lines from Rebecca Rogers's stone:

> From chimney-money too this cell is free:
> To such a House as this who would not tenant be.

In tombstone inscriptions and epitaphs life has many metaphorical comparisons as at **Heanor,** Derbyshire, in the epitaph to William Brough (1815):

> What is life? a Breath; a Dream;
> A Bubble in a rapid Stream;
> A lurid Shade, with scarce a ray;
> A Short and Stormy Winter's day;
> A falling Star; a morning Flower;
> A passing Cloud, an Autumn Shower.
> A flying Shuttle, nay a Span;
> So short and frail's the Life of Man.

A tomb at **Zennor,** Cornwall, shows life represented by four winds, with a pointer directing the reader (1790):

> Hope, Fear, False joy and trouble,
> Are those four winds which daily toss this bubble,
> His breath's a vapour and his Life's a span,
> 'Tis glorious Misery to be born a Man.

The commonly-used couplet,

> As I am now, so you must be,
> Therefore prepare to follow me,

has added to it, in **Woolwich** churchyard, this witticism:

> To follow you I'm not content
> Until I know which way you went.

Bangor, in Wales, has an epitaph which touches on the medical history of the deceased:

> Poor Marth Snell, her's gone away,
> Her would if her could, but her couldn't stay.
> Her had two bad legs and a baddish cough,
> But her legs it was that carried her off.

Anagrams

Occasionally one may encounter epitaphs which include anagrams. At **St. Ives,** Cornwall, is a memorial to six members of the Sise family:

> Neere to this bed sixe Sises late wer laid,
> Foure hopefull sonns, a grandsire, and a maid,
> All striving which should end his journey first
> All for the well-spring of true life did thirst:
> The virgin's elegy outweepes the rest,
> Such lovely grase was stampt on face and brest.

Then this anagram commemorates the maid, Alice Sise, died 1642:

> ALICE SISE : ILLS CEASE

Another example, this one from **Lyme Regis,** Dorset, dating from 1636, takes a certain liberty with the spelling:

> ELIZABET: ROSE
>
> Anag.
>
> OHE BLEST ARISE
> OH BLEST in faith, in life, in death,
> In husband and posterytye,
> ARISE to everlasting Joye
> And blessed immortalitie.

So have been recorded, on thousands of tombstones the length and breadth of the country, the virtues and faults of our ancestors, their trades and professions, their interests and eccentricities, their families, and their own little lives which 'have ended in sleep'. The best epitaphs are those in the churchyards of villages and country towns and few were written by great poets or preachers. The monumental mason carved out of the native stone or slate the inscriptions to the departed, not always sure of spelling or of grammar. Many are vanished; many more are steadily flaking away in our English weather; those that remain need to be recorded before it is too late.

If you seek epitaphs please remember to treat churchyards with reverence, and tread quietly, remembering Shakespeare's own warning, on his tomb in the parish church at **Stratford-upon-Avon:**

> Good friend, for Jes's sake forbeare
> To digg the dust enclosed heare;
> Blessed be ye man yt spares these stones,
> And curst be he yt moves my bones.

GAZETTEER

Of the thousands of churchyards in the country, only about 200 have been mentioned in the text. This does not mean that the others have nothing to offer, but simply that one person cannot, even over a number of years, do more than just scratch the surface. Those mentioned in the text are given here, as well as others which have something worth seeing, either epitaph, lettering quality, monumental sculpture, or just 'atmosphere'. But the list does not claim to be either exhaustive or comprehensive.

ENGLAND

Bedfordshire: Luton, Turvey.

Berkshire: Basildon, Bray, Buckland, Childrey, Cold Ash, Compton Beauchamp, Faringdon, Letcombe Regis, Wantage, Winkfield.

Bristol: Brislington, Henbury.

Buckinghamshire: Beaconsfield, Fingest, Hanslope, Marsworth, Olney, Shabbington, Upton, West Wycombe.

Cambridgeshire: Sawston.

Cheshire: Disley.

Cornwall: Madron, Rock, St. Endellion, St. Ives, St. Just in Penwith, St. Merryn, St. Minver, St. Teath, Saltash, Zennor.

Cumberland: Keswick, Workington.

Derbyshire: Bakewell, Heanor, Wirksworth.

Devon: Appledore, Bideford, Bridestowe, Kingsbridge, Lydford, West Down, Widecombe-in-the-Moor.

Dorset: Blandford Forum, Bridport, Farnham, Lyme Regis, Portesham, Portland, Winterborne Stickland.

Durham: Monkwearmouth, Seaham.

Essex: Bradfield, Birdbrook, Brightlingsea, Colchester, Great Bentley, Great Bromley, Hadleigh, Hatfield Broad Oak, High Easter, Little Easton, Mistley, Ramsey, Weeley.

Gloucestershire: Ampney Crucis, Awre, Barnsley, Berkeley, Bisley, Bourton-on-the-Water, Chipping Sodbury, Cirencester, Daylesford, Dumbleton, Eastleach Martin, Elmore, Frampton-on-Severn, Hardwicke, Kingscote, Little Dean, Lydney, Miserden, Newnham-on-Severn, Oddington, Painswick, Pebworth, Sapperton, Standish, Tetbury, Westbury, Winchcombe, Withington.

Hampshire: North Stoneham, Petersfield, Winchester.

Herefordshire: Sarnesfield.

Hertfordshire: Barley, New Mill, North Mimms.

Huntingdon and Peterborough: Old Weston, Peterborough.

Kent: Folkestone, Frindsbury, Great Chart, Hothfield, Minster-in-Sheppey, Ramsgate, Sutton-at-Hone.

Lancashire: Blackpool, Cartmel Fell, Lindale-in-Cartmel, Liverpool.

Leicestershire: Ashby Folville, Breedon-on-the-Hill, Burbage, Burton Lazars, Burton Overy, Edmondthorpe, Gilmorton, Great Dalby, Loughborough, Melton Mowbray, Normanton, Old Dalby, Rothley, Stanford-on-Soar, Swithland, Wymeswold, Wymondham.

Lincolnshire: Spalding.

London (Greater): Beckenham, Crayford, Edmonton, Hammersmith, Hampstead, Highgate, Hillingdon, Lambeth, St. Paul's, Stoke Newington, Twickenham, Westminster, Woolwich.

Norfolk: Great Yarmouth, Norwich, Woodton.

Northamptonshire: Finedon, Oundle, Yarwell.

Northumberland: Alnwick.

Nottinghamshire: Bingham, Farndon, Hickling, Nottingham, Rempstone.

Oxfordshire: Bampton, Beckley, Bladon, Burford, Charlton-on-Otmoor, Dorchester, Islip, Kelmscott, Kirtlington, Lewknor, Stadhampton, Stanton Harcourt, Thame, Waterperry.

Rutland: Belton.

Shropshire: Broseley, Coalbrookdale, Heath, Madeley, More.

Somerset: Bath, Berrow, Bishop's Lydeard, Easton-in-Gordano, Farleigh Hungerford, Kilmersdon, Muchelney, Pilton, Street, Watchet, West Pennard.

Staffordshire: Colton, Longnor, Stoke-on-Trent, Wolstanton.

Suffolk: Belstead, Bury St. Edmunds, Lavenham, Leiston, Long Melford, Palgrave, Rendlesham, Southwold, Stanstead, Westleton.

Surrey: Betchworth, Chobham, Crowhurst, Esher, Ockham.

Sussex: Battle, Bosham, Brightling, East Grinstead, Lewes, Rotherfield, Sidlesham, Wadhurst, Westbourne.

Warwickshire: Coventry, Stratford-upon-Avon.

Westmorland: Troutbeck.

Wiltshire: Bishopstone, Bremhill, Burbage, Corsham, Devizes, Donhead St. Mary, Easterton, Easton Grey, Great Bedwyn, Hardenhuish, Lydiard Tregoze, Malmesbury, Potterne, Stanton St. Quintin, Swindon, Tockenham, Wroughton, Wylye.

Worcestershire: Belbroughton, Broadway, Bromsgrove, Childswickham, Church Honeybourne, Cleeve Prior, Evesham, Pershore, Shrawley, Upton-upon-Severn.

Yorkshire: Beverley, Bolton-on-Swale, Bridlington, Croft, Gilling, Keighley, Kildwick, Kirby Hill, Marton, Masham, Otley, Ripon, Saddleworth, Spofforth, Thornton Steward, West Linton, Whitby.

SCOTLAND

Anwoth, Edinburgh, Gatehouse of Fleet, New Galloway.

WALES

Bangor, Holyhead, Llandovery, Llanfair Discoed, Llanvetherine, Montgomery.

BIBLIOGRAPHY

A Book of Epitaphs; Raymond L. Brown; David and Charles, 1969.
English Churchyard Memorials; F. Burgess; Lutterworth, 1963.
Of Graves and Epitaphs; Kenneth Lindley; Hutchinson, 1965.

FINIS.

INDEX